SPELLING FOR MINECRAFTERS

Grade 4

Illustrated by Amanda Brack

Sky Pony Press
New York

Sky Pony Press books may be purchased in bulk at special discounts for sales promotion, corporate gifts, fund-raising, or educational purposes. Special editions can also be created to specifications. For details, contact the Special Sales Department, Sky Pony Press, 307 West 36th Street, 11th Floor, New York, NY 10018 or info@skyhorsepublishing.com.

Sky Pony® is a registered trademark of Skyhorse Publishing, Inc.®, a Delaware corporation.

Visit our website at www.skyponypress.com.

Authors, books, and more at SkyPonyPressBlog.com.

10 9 8 7 6 5 4 3 2 1

Library of Congress Cataloging-in-Publication Data is available on file.

Cover design by Brian Peterson

Cover illustration by Bill Greenhead

Interior illustrations by Amanda Brack

Book design by Kevin Baier

Print ISBN: 978-1-5107-4112-6

Printed in China

A NOTE TO PARENTS

When you want to reinforce classroom skills at home, it's crucial to have kid-friendly learning materials. This *Spelling for Minecrafters* workbook transforms spelling practice into an irresistible adventure, complete with diamond swords, zombies, skeletons, and creepers. That means less arguing over homework and more fun overall.

Spelling for Minecrafters is also fully aligned with National Common Core Standards for 4th-grade spelling. What does that mean, exactly? All of the spelling skills taught in this book correspond to what your child is expected to learn in school. This eliminates confusion and builds confidence for greater homework-time success!

Whether it's the joy of seeing their favorite game characters on every page or the thrill of spelling with Steve and Alex, there is something in this workbook to entice even the most reluctant speller.

Happy adventuring!

STRANGE ENDINGS

*When you see 'aught' or 'ought' at the end of a word, it is sometimes pronounced **ot**. Use the box of words to complete the sentences.*

| fought | bought | taught | caught | onslaught |

1. The villager _____ all my loot and gave me some valuable items in return.

2. Steve _____ a pufferfish at the lake.

3. I was attacked in the Nether by an _____ of zombie pigmen.

4. I _____ my sister how to tame a wolf with bones.

5. Alex _____ a trio of arrow-slinging skeletons.

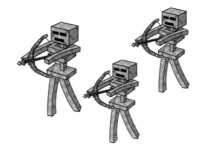

ACHIEVEMENT LIST

Make a list of your Minecrafting accomplishments below. Have you caught a rare fish, played in survival mode, or taught yourself how to make a redstone trap? Use as many 'ght' words from the box as you can.

fought	bought	taught	caught	onslaught

1. _____

_____

2. _____

_____

3. _____

_____

4. _____

_____

5. _____

_____

ORDER CHALLENGE

*Practice spelling the sight words below as you write them on the lines in **alphabetical order** from top to bottom.*

| before | actually | brought | against | among | busy |

1. _____

2. _____

3. _____

4. _____

5. _____

6. _____

SIGHT WORD FILL-IN

Use the box of words to finish the sentences below.

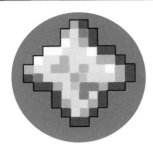

before	actually	brought	against	among	busy

1. I can't believe I _____ defeated the Wither and collected a Nether star!

2. I _____ all of my Ender pearls with me when I traveled to the End.

3. The witch hut was nestled _____ the trees in the Swamp Biome.

4. I heard a zombie bang _____ my wooden door.

5. Collect lots of soul sand _____ you leave the Nether.

6. I was so _____ building a bed that I didn't notice an approaching creeper.

STEVE'S WORD SCRAMBLE

Unscramble the words below, and write them correctly on the line. Then count the number of syllables and write the number on the line.

NUMBER OF SYLLABLES

1. syub   _____   _____

2. gubroth   _____   _____

3. tuylaalc   _____   _____

4. goamn   _____   _____

5. tainsga   _____   _____

6. ebreof   _____   _____

POLAR BEAR'S PREFIX CHALLENGE

Adding a prefix to the beginning of a root word can change the word's meaning. The prefixes dis, im, *and* in *mean* **'not'** *when added to the beginning of the words below. Write the new meaning of the word on the line. The first one is done for you.*

	PREFIX		ROOT WORD		NEW WORD	NEW MEANING
1.	dis	+	like	=	dislike	not like
2.	dis	+	appear	=	_____	_____
3.	in	+	correct	=	_____	_____
4.	in	+	sane	=	_____	_____
5.	im	+	patient	=	_____	_____
6.	dis	+	agree	=	_____	_____

FIND-THE-PREFIX

Read the sentence. Guess the meaning of the word in bold using the context clues and the prefix to help you.

1. There's a potion in Minecraft that makes a player **invisible**.

Meaning: _____

2. It's almost **impossible** to kill the Ender Dragon on your

first try.

Meaning: _____

3. Raw chorus fruit can be eaten, but popped chorus fruit

is **inedible**.

Meaning: _____

4. If minecart tracks are **disconnected**, your railway system

won't work.

Meaning: _____

5. If your parents are extremely **uninterested** in Minecraft,

you are not alone!

Meaning: _____

RAINBOW WRITING

Practice spelling the sight words below. First, write each word in pencil. Then trace over the letters three times with a different colored pencil each time.

| built | certain | compare | complete | close | possible |

1. _____

2. _____

3. _____

4. _____

5. _____

6. _____

DEAR FELLOW GAMER

Write a short letter to your best friend telling him/her about the last thing you built in Minecraft and what you've learned about building in Minecraft. Your challenge: use as many of the sight words below as you can.

built	certain	compare	complete	close	possible

Dear _____,

_____

_____

_____

_____

_____

_____

_____

Sincerely,

_____

GHASTLY SPELLING ERRORS

Look for one spelling mistake in each sentence below. Cross out the mistake and write the word correctly on the line.

1. I should have bilt my house out of cobblestone.

_____

2. I'm certen that I have enough Eyes of Ender to build a portal.

_____

3. It's hard to compair creative and survival mode in Minecraft: They're both good in different ways.

_____

4. Try to compleet your shelter before nightfall so you don't get attacked by hostile mobs.

_____

5. I was really clous to beating the Ender Dragon today.

_____

6. Anything is posible when you're building in Minecraft.

_____

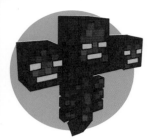

WITHER'S WORD SEARCH

Can you find and circle all the words from the list?

built	against	compare
before	among	complete
actually	busy	close
brought	certain	possible

```
C E R T A I N A L E N X
Q A N E G P C C L O S E
C D G N R T N B T T N M
N O O A U A I P H L Z J
Q M M A I S P G B E J W
A T L P S N U M R J D G
G L R O L O S O O B J Z
Y I P X R E F T U C Y Q
K U N B X E T S Y B M N
Q B B T B Y Y E Q J Q L
```

EVOKER'S VOWEL PAIRS

Match the vowel team 'ea' word to the picture it best describes. Circle the words where 'ea' make a long vowel sound. Underline the words where 'ea' makes a short vowel sound.

1. scream

2. thread

3. leather armor

4. feather

5. beasts

6. breathe

SIGHT WORD FILL-IN

Use the box of "ea" words to finish the sentences below.

ready	meat	breathe	feather	beasts	scream

1. Cows and mooshrooms drop 0 to 2 pieces of _____ when they're destroyed.

2. To build an arrow, you'll need flint, a stick, and a white _____.

3. The Wither is one of the most dangerous _____ in the game.

4. You can hear a ghast _____ from very far away.

5. With the right potion, you can _____ underwater.

6. When you travel through a portal to the End, you had better be _____ to fight.

CREEPER'S CROSSWORD

Use the list below and the word provided to fill in the rest of the puzzle.

during

describe

measure

~~decision~~

different

develop

CREEPER'S WORD LADDER

Solve this word ladder using the clues provided. Start with the word at the bottom and move your way up the ladder.

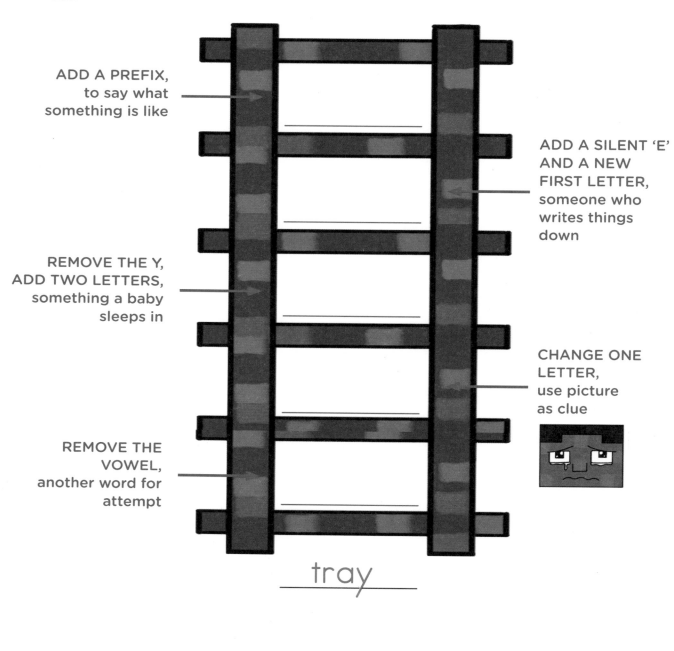

ADD A PREFIX, to say what something is like

ADD A SILENT 'E' AND A NEW FIRST LETTER, someone who writes things down

REMOVE THE Y, ADD TWO LETTERS, something a baby sleeps in

CHANGE ONE LETTER, use picture as clue

REMOVE THE VOWEL, another word for attempt

tray

DEAR TEACHER

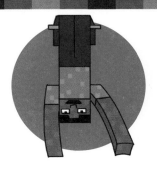

Write a short letter to your teacher trying to convince her that Minecrafting should be a school subject. Your challenge: use as many of the sight words below as you can.

describe	decision	measure	develop	different	during

Dear Teacher,

_____

_____

_____

_____

_____

_____

_____

Sincerely,

_____

CAVE SPIDER SCRAMBLE

Unscramble the words below using the clues provided.

1. eesdcrib _____ to say what something looks like

2. iodencis _____ a choice you have to make

3. emasure _____ to find the length of something

4. podleve _____ to grow

5. fifendter _____ not the same

6. gruidn _____ at the same time

VOWEL PAIR IE AND EI

Vowel pair ie and ei shows up in a lot of words. To remember which order to put them in, remember the rhyme: **i before e except after c.**

Write ie or ei in the space provided to make a word. Use the rule above to guide you.

1. p __ __ ce

2. p __ __ rce

3. bel __ __ ve

4. c __ __ ling

5. rec __ __ ve

6. ach __ __ ve

FISHING FOR THE RIGHT WORD

Fill in the blanks with the correct 'ie' or 'ei' word.

pierce	believe	achieve	received	pieces	ceiling

1. My sword is sharp enough to _____ a zombie.

2. I don't _____ my brother when he says he defeated

the Wither on the first try.

3. Making a cake in Minecraft is one goal I want to _____.

4. I once made a Minecraft fortress with an iron ore _____.

5. I gave the villager one emerald and _____ ten

_____ of leather in return.

BUILDING WORDS

Practice spelling the sight words. Start with the word with the fewest letters, writing the words in the blocks below in order **from shortest to longest** word. If two words have the same number of letters, put them in alphabetical order.

| daily | easy | either | else | familiar | themselves |

1. ☐ ☐ ☐ ☐

2. ☐ ☐ ☐ ☐

3. ☐ ☐ ☐ ☐ ☐

4. ☐ ☐ ☐ ☐ ☐ ☐

5. ☐ ☐ ☐ ☐ ☐ ☐ ☐ ☐

6. ☐ ☐ ☐ ☐ ☐ ☐ ☐ ☐ ☐ ☐

GHASTLY SPELLING ERRORS

Look for one spelling mistake in each sentence below. Cross out the mistake and write the word correctly on the line. Be sure to include capital letters at the start of sentences.

1. I can play eather hardcore mode or easy mode.

_____

2. Attacking sheeps, pigs, and horses is very eesy.

_____

3. I'm familar with all the mobs that live in the Nether.

_____

4. Zombies sometimes fall off ledges and destroy themself.

_____

5. You better know how to survive the first night in Minecraft, or elce.

_____

6. This game feels like it gets updated dayly.

_____

MOOSHROOM MATCH

Match the sight word to its meaning. Then write a sentence using one of the sight words.

1. daily   the opposite of difficult

2. easy   recognizable, not new

3. either   every day

4. familiar   a reflexive pronoun for *they*

5. themselves   one or the other

_____

_____

_____

WITCH'S WORD BUILDER

*A suffix appears at the end of a root word and changes its meaning. The suffix **-able** is usually used when the root word is already a complete word. The suffix **–ible** is usually used when the root is not a complete word. Make new words below by adding the suffix **-ible** or **-able**.*

	IBLE OR ABLE	NEW WORD
1. comfort	_____	_____
2. notice	_____	_____
3. poss	_____	_____
4. vis	_____	_____
5. terr	_____	_____
6. agree	_____	_____

READY TO WRITE

Circle three qualities from the word box below that best describe you. Add your own words if you think of any. On the lines provided, explain why these words describe you.

flexible	lovable	noticeable	agreeable
incredible	remarkable	unstoppable	knowledgeable

RAINBOW WRITING

Write the sight words in alphabetical order on the lines below. Then trace over the letters three times with a different colored pencil each time.

interest	half	heart	instead	tried	heavy

1. _____

2. _____

3. _____

4. _____

5. _____

6. _____

OCELOT'S WORD PROWL

Use the box of words below to complete the sentences.

interest	half	hearts	instead	tried	heavy

1. The _____ anvil fell on the creeper's head.

2. Iron golems have no _____ in attacking passive mobs.

3. A full health bar has ten _____.

4. If you take damage, you can lose _____ a heart or a whole heart.

5. If you want to get wood from a tree, use an axe _____ of a sword.

6. I _____ to run away from the Enderman, but he was too fast.

WOLFY'S WORD SEARCH

Can you find and circle all the words from the list?

daily	familiar	instead
easy	themselves	hearts
either	interest	tried
else	half	heavy

```
T X K H E A R T S E
H I H A L F N T S R
E N F I T Y D L E G
M T D A N V E H N D
S E E E M S T D A M
E R I A D I T I H M
L E R S E W L E K L
V S T Y L Y A I A B
E T W M G V T J A D
S N K N Y W M Q M R
```

GUARDIAN'S GLIDING VOWELS

A gliding vowel (also called a **diphthong**) occurs when a combination of two vowel sounds occur in one syllable. The first vowel sound glides into the next. Use the gliding vowel combinations below to complete the words in the sentences.

oi	oy	ou	ow

1. You can destr___ ___ a zombie with a diamond sword.

2. A ghast makes a n___ ___se that sounds like a scream.

3. To get a c___ ___ to follow you, hold out some wheat.

4. You can build a h___ ___se out of anything in Minecraft.

Write your own Minecrafting sentence using a word with a gliding vowel.

_____

_____

_____

POTION OF POETRY WRITING

Sip a potion of poetry writing and give this fun activity a try! Think of a word with the same gliding vowel sound to complete these rhyming verses.

1. Wither, Wither in the sky,

when I see you I start to _____.

2. Lots of mushrooms can be found

in the Nether on the _____.

3. That ocelot that's standing there

gave the creeper an awful _____.

4. I only have half an hour

before my laptop runs out of _____.

5. If I could I'd like to play

Minecraft each and every _____.

BUILDING WORDS

Practice spelling the sight words. Start with the word with the fewest letters, writing the words on the boxes in order from shortest to longest word. If two words have the same number of letters, put them in alphabetical order.

kept	together	leave	near	might	people

1. ☐☐☐☐

2. ☐☐☐☐

3. ☐☐☐☐☐

4. ☐☐☐☐☐

5. ☐☐☐☐☐☐

6. ☐☐☐☐☐☐☐☐

DEAR VILLAGERS

Write a short letter to Minecraft villagers whose village is about to be attacked by zombies. Tell them why they should leave right away. Your challenge: use as many of the sight words below as you can.

kept	together	leave	near	might	people

Dear Villagers,

_____

_____

_____

_____

_____

_____

_____

Sincerely,

_____

FIND AND FIX

Look for one spelling mistake in each sentence below. Cross out the mistake and write the word correctly on the line.

1. I keppt all of my diamonds hidden in a chest. _____

2. We can defeat a skeleton army if we work tugethur. _____

3. There are lots of peepul who play Minecraft. _____

4. Try not to build a home neer grass if you want to start a wheat farm. _____

5. Don't leive your home at night without a torch. _____

6. If you travel to the savanna, you mite run into llamas. _____

CRAFTER'S CROSSWORD

When you join two words together, you can make a **compound word**, *like butterfly. Use the list of compound words below and the word provided to fill in the rest of the crossword puzzle.*

fireball   snowman   ~~watermelon~~

everybody   overworld   tripwire

minecart

BUILDING COMPOUNDS

What smaller word is missing from each **compound word**?
Fill in the blanks to complete the word. Use the picture
clues to help.

1. Running through a cob_____ makes me

   go slower.

2. A day_____ sensor can automatically

   close your doors at night to keep mobs out.

3. Use a _____stone torch to power your

   next trap.

4. When you need a source of light,

   glow_____ blocks are very useful.

5. Eating _____ fish can be hazardous to

   your health.

WORD SPAWNER

Match a Minecrafting word in the left column with a word in the right column to make a new, silly, compound word. Add a definition and a picture.

zombie	ball
lava	hat
spawn	stone
Nether	axe
melon	jockey

My new word: _____ + _____ =

_____

What it means: _____

_____

_____

What it looks like:

RAINBOW WRITING

Practice spelling the sight words below. First, write each word in pencil. Then trace over the letters three times with a different colored pencil each time.

receive	reason	scared	several	should	shown

1. _____

2. _____

3. _____

4. _____

5. _____

6. _____

DEAR PARENTS

Imagine how much fun it would be to have a pet creeper! Write a short letter to your parents giving them reasons to let you keep your favorite mob as a pet. Your challenge: use as many of the sight words below as you can.

receive	reason	scared	several	should	shown

Dear Mom/Dad,

_____

_____

_____

_____

_____

_____

_____

_____

Sincerely,

_____

EVOKER'S WORD SCRAMBLE

Unscramble the words below, and write them correctly on the line. (Hint: Choose from the sight words on page 38.)

1. I **evercie** _____ sixteen carrots from

a farmer villager.

2. The villager is **darces** _____ of

zombie attacks.

3. I can list a thousand **seraons** _____ why

Minecraft is the best game ever.

4. There are **veerals** _____ kinds of

potions a player can brew.

5. Before you battle a ghast, you **holdus**

_____ build a snow golem to help you.

SILENT LETTERS

B is silent after m and before t. Which of these words have a silent b? Circle them.

dab	timber	robe
crumb	thumb	doubt
noob	orb	climb

Write a sentence with a silent b word below:

_____

_____

_____

_____

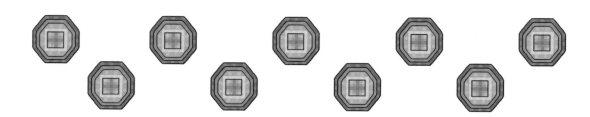

FISHY FILL-IN

Fill in the blank spaces below with a word that has a silent letter. Use the word box to help you.

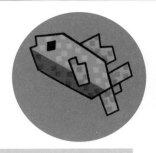

climb	doubt	wrong	limbs	wraps

1. Giant oaks are one of the few trees in Minecraft that have

_____.

2. One _____ move in the Nether and you

could fall into a lava pit!

3. I had no _____ that I would find my way back

to the Nether portal.

4. Creepers are not able to _____ ladders.

5. A skin is a file that _____ around a player

and changes its appearance.

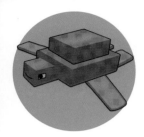

ORDER CHALLENGE

Practice spelling the sight words below as you write them on the lines in alphabetical order from top to bottom.

| sincerely | someone | through | simple | since | special |

1. _____

2. _____

3. _____

4. _____

5. _____

6. _____

WITHER SKELETON'S WORD SEARCH

Can you find and circle all the words from the list?

simple	someone	receive	several
since	special	reason	should
sincerely	through	scared	shown

```
T H R O U G H N W O H S S X
S T N O S A E R V L B O X R
I J D R N I G D Q R M Y Y M
N J Y P T B M M E E W L B D
C D L J Y D M P O R L V Z D
E D E J K V Y N L A A Y N P
Q L R E M Z E S R E S C L B
T R E X V P Y E P H Y M S Y
N Y C B M I V Q O E K K V R
Y L N B P E E U K T C D B L
Q N I L S B L C R G P I R V
N N S R N D X M E L T B A D
X N V K Q L M M R R Y Z L L
```

ALEX'S WORD LADDER

Solve this word ladder using the clues provided. Start with the word at the bottom and move your way up the ladder.

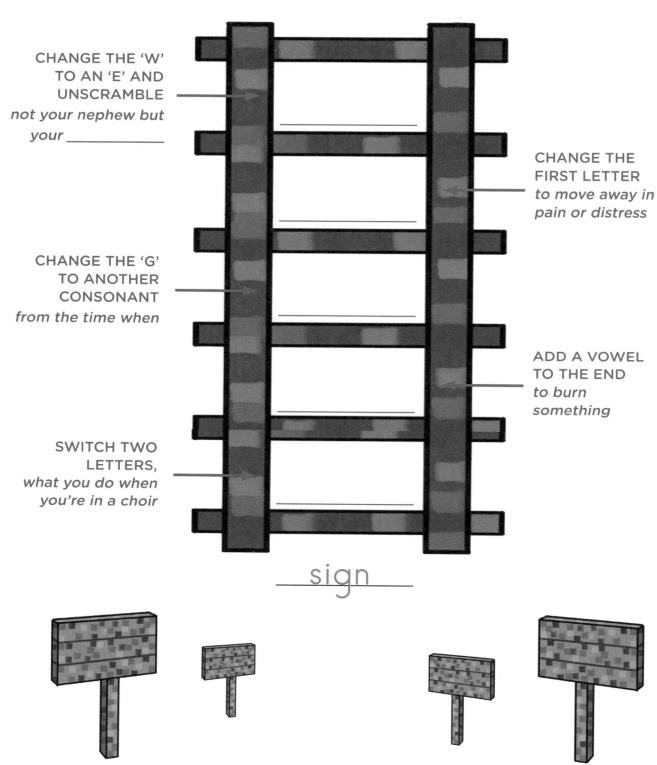

CHANGE THE 'W' TO AN 'E' AND UNSCRAMBLE
not your nephew but your _____

CHANGE THE 'G' TO ANOTHER CONSONANT
from the time when

SWITCH TWO LETTERS,
what you do when you're in a choir

CHANGE THE FIRST LETTER
to move away in pain or distress

ADD A VOWEL TO THE END
to burn something

sign

DEAR MINECRAFT CREATOR

Write a short letter to the creator of Minecraft. Explain what you think is special about the game, ask questions, or make suggestions for improving the game. Your challenge: use as many of the sight words below as you can.

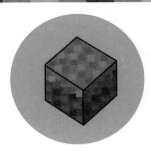

simple	since	someone	special	through

Dear Minecraft Creator,

_____

_____

_____

_____

_____

_____

_____

Sincerely,

_____

FIND AND FIX

Look for one spelling mistake in each sentence below. Cross out the mistake and write the word correctly on the line.

1. A sponge is a spechul block that you can find in an ocean monument.   _____

2. A griefer is somewon who likes to trick other players.   _____

3. It's been days sinze I last played Minecraft.   _____

4. A mob farm is a simpul way to collect useful items.   _____

5. Water can flow thru a trap door.   _____

PLURAL NOUN PRACTICE

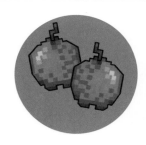

When a noun ends with a vowel + y, you can add an 's' to make it plural. When a noun ends in consonant + y, change the 'y' to 'i' and add 'es.' Look at each word below and write its plural form on the space provided.

1. donkey  _____

2. family _____

3. chimney 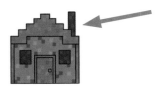 _____

4. party  _____

5. butterfly _____

DEAR ALEX

Write a short letter to Alex telling her about the Minecraft farm you want to create and how you would feed and protect the animals. Your challenge: use as many of the plural words below as you can.

bunnies   donkeys   puppies   ponies   supplies   enemies

Dear Alex,

_____

_____

_____

_____

_____

_____

_____

_____

Sincerely,

_____

BUILDING WORDS

Practice spelling the plural words ending in 's' or 'ies'. Start with the word with the fewest letters, writing the words on the boxes in order from shortest to longest word. If two words have the same number of letters, put them in alphabetical order.

cities   surveys   holidays   toys   melodies   pennies

1. ☐ ☐ ☐ ☐

2. ☐ ☐ ☐ ☐ ☐ ☐

3. ☐ ☐ ☐ ☐ ☐ ☐ ☐

4. ☐ ☐ ☐ ☐ ☐ ☐ ☐

5. ☐ ☐ ☐ ☐ ☐ ☐ ☐ ☐

6. ☐ ☐ ☐ ☐ ☐ ☐ ☐ ☐

SIGHT WORD REVIEW: COPY AND LEARN

Copy the words on the lines provided.

1. before _____

2. actually _____

3. brought _____

4. against _____

5. among _____

6. busy _____

7. built _____

8. certain _____

9. compare _____

10. complete _____

11. close _____

12. possible _____

SPELLING TEST 1: SIGHT WORDS

*Time to do some wordcrafting! Have a parent or friend read the words from **page 50** to you and see how many you can spell correctly.*

Date:

_____

Number correct:

_____

1. _____

2. _____

3. _____

4. _____

5. _____

6. _____

7. _____

8. _____

9. _____

10. _____

11. _____

12. _____

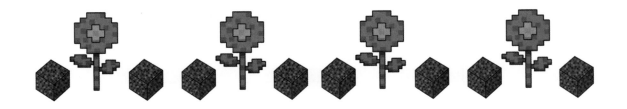

SIGHT WORD REVIEW: COPY AND LEARN

Copy the words on the lines provided.

1. describe   _____

2. decision   _____

3. measure   _____

4. develop   _____

5. different   _____

6. during   _____

7. daily   _____

8. easy   _____

9. either   _____

10. else   _____

11. familiar   _____

12. themselves   _____

SPELLING TEST 2: SIGHT WORDS

*Time to do some wordcrafting! Have a parent or friend read the words from **page 52** to you and see how many you can spell correctly.*

Date:

_____

Number correct:

_____

1. _____

2. _____

3. _____

4. _____

5. _____

6. _____

7. _____

8. _____

9. _____

10. _____

11. _____

12. _____

SIGHT WORD REVIEW: COPY AND LEARN

Copy the words on the lines provided.

1. interest _____

2. half _____

3. heart _____

4. instead _____

5. tried _____

6. heavy _____

7. kept _____

8. together _____

9. leave _____

10. near _____

11. might _____

12. people _____

SPELLING TEST 3: SIGHT WORDS

*Time to do some wordcrafting! Have a parent or friend read the words from **page 54** to you and see how many you can spell correctly.*

Date:

_____

Number correct:

_____

1. _____

2. _____

3. _____

4. _____

5. _____

6. _____

7. _____

8. _____

9. _____

10. _____

11. _____

12. _____

SIGHT WORD REVIEW: COPY AND LEARN

Copy the words on the lines provided.

1. receive _____

2. reason _____

3. scared _____

4. several _____

5. should _____

6. shown _____

7. sincerely _____

8. someone _____

9. through _____

10. simple _____

11. since _____

12. special _____

SPELLING TEST 4: SIGHT WORDS

*Time to do some wordcrafting! Have a parent or friend read the words from **page 56** to you and see how many you can spell correctly.*

Date:

_____

Number correct:

_____

1. _____

2. _____

3. _____

4. _____

5. _____

6. _____

7. _____

8. _____

9. _____

10. _____

11. _____

12. _____

ANSWERS

STRANGE ENDINGS
PAGE 2

1. bought
2. caught
3. onslaught
4. taught
5. fought

ACHIEVEMENT LIST
PAGE 3

Answers will vary.

ORDER CHALLENGE
PAGE 4

1. actually
2. against
3. among
4. before
5. brought
6. busy

SIGHT WORD FILL-IN
PAGE 5

1. actually
2. brought
3. among
4. against
5. before
6. busy

STEVE'S WORD SCRAMBLE
PAGE 6

1. busy   2
2. brought   1
3. actually   3
4. among   2
5. against   2
6. before   2

POLAR BEAR'S PREFIX CHALLENGE
PAGE 7

2. disappear   not there
3. incorrect   not right
4. insane   not sane
5. impatient   not patient
6. disagree   don't agree

FIND-THE-PREFIX
PAGE 8

1. invisible   can't see it
2. impossible   can't do
3. inedible   can't eat
4. disconnected   not connected
5. uninterested   not interested

RAINBOW WRITING
PAGE 9

1. built
2. certain
3. compare
4. complete
5. close
6. possible

DEAR FELLOW GAMER
PAGE 10

Answers will vary.

GHASTLY SPELLING ERRORS
PAGE 11

1. built
2. certain
3. compare
4. complete
5. close
6. possible

WITHER'S WORD SEARCH
PAGE 12

EVOKER'S VOWEL PAIRS
PAGE 13

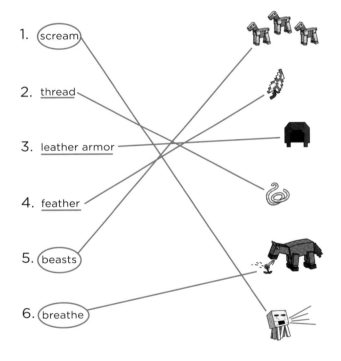

1. scream
2. thread
3. leather armor
4. feather
5. beasts
6. breathe

SIGHT WORD FILL-IN
PAGE 14

1. meat
2. feather
3. beasts
4. scream
5. breathe
6. ready

CREEPER'S CROSSWORD PUZZLE
PAGE 15

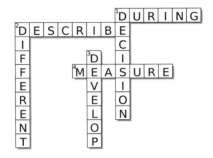

CREEPER'S WORD LADDER
PAGE 16

describe

scribe

crib

cry

try

DEAR TEACHER
PAGE 17

Answers will vary.

CAVE SPIDER SCRAMBLE
PAGE 18

1. describe
2. decision
3. measure
4. develop
5. different
6. during

VOWEL PAIR IE AND EI
PAGE 19

1. piece
2. pierce
3. believe
4. ceiling
5. receive
6. achieve

FISHING FOR THE RIGHT WORD
PAGE 20
1. pierce
2. believe
3. achieve
4. ceiling
5. received, pieces

BUILDING WORDS
PAGE 21
1. easy
2. else
3. daily
4. either
5. familiar
6. themselves

GHASTLY SPELLING ERRORS
PAGE 22
1. either
2. easy
3. familiar
4. themselves
5. else
6. daily

MOOSHROOM MATCH
PAGE 23
1. daily is matched to every day
2. easy is matched with the opposite of difficult
3. either is matched with one or the other
4. familiar is matched with recognizable, not new
5. themselves is matched with a reflexive pronoun for they
Answers will vary.

WITCH'S WORD BUILDER
PAGE 24
1. able   comfortable
2. able   noticeable
3. ible   possible
4. ible   visible
5. ible   terrible
6. able   agreeable

READY TO WRITE
PAGE 25
Answers will vary.

RAINBOW WRITING
PAGE 26
1. half
2. heart
3. heavy
4. instead
5. interest
6. tried

OCELOT'S WORD PROWL
PAGE 27
1. heavy
2. interest
3. hearts
4. half
5. instead
6. tried

WOLFY'S WORD SEARCH
PAGE 28

GUARDIAN'S GLIDING VOWELS
PAGE 29

1. oy
2. oi
3. ow
4. ou

Answers will vary.

POTION OF POETRY WRITING
PAGE 30

1. cry
2. ground
3. stare
4. power
5. day

BUILDING WORDS
PAGE 31

1. kept
2. near
3. leave
4. might
5. people
6. together

DEAR VILLAGERS
PAGE 32

Answers will vary.

FIND AND FIX
PAGE 33

1. kept
2. together
3. people
4. near
5. leave
6. might

CRAFTER'S CROSSWORD
PAGE 34

BUILDING COMPOUNDS
PAGE 35

1. web
2. light
3. red
4. stone
5. puffer

WORD SPAWNER
PAGE 36

Answers will vary.

RAINBOW WRITING
PAGE 37

reason
receive
scared
several
should
shown

DEAR PARENTS
PAGE 38

Answers will vary.

EVOKER'S WORD SCRAMBLE
PAGE 39

1. receive
2. scared
3. reasons
4. several
5. should

SILENT LETTERS
PAGE 40

dab   timber   robe

(crumb)   (thumb)   (doubt)

noob   orb   (climb)

FISHY FILL-IN, PAGE 41

1. Giant oaks are one of the few trees in Minecraft that have limbs.
2. One wrong move in the Nether and you could fall into a lava pit!
3. I had no doubt that I would find my way back to the Nether portal.
4. Creepers are not able to climb ladders.
5. A skin is a file that wraps around a player and changes its appearance.

ORDER CHALLENGE
PAGE 42

1. simple
2. since
3. sincerely
4. someone
5. special
6. through

WITHER SKELETON'S WORD SEARCH
PAGE 43

ALEX'S WORD LADDER
PAGE 44

niece
wince
since
singe
sing
sign

DEAR MINECRAFT CREATOR
PAGE 45

Answers will vary.

FIND AND FIX
PAGE 46

1. special
2. someone
3. since
4. simple
5. through

PLURAL NOUN PRACTICE
PAGE 47

1. donkeys
2. families
3. chimneys
4. parties
5. butterflies

DEAR ALEX
PAGE 48

Answers may vary.

BUILDING WORDS
PAGE 49

1. toys
2. cities
3. pennies
4. surveys
5. holidays
6. melodies